C O N T E N T S

THE FIVE-MINUTE PROBLEM SOLVER

How many problems do you face during a normal day? Have you ever counted? Oh, well, why bother. It wouldn't reduce the number anyway.

From the moment you wake up in the morning until you go to bed at night, you are faced with decisions. What should I wear? What should I eat for breakfast? Or, maybe no breakfast. Can I take the day off, or will the work pile up the next day, and I'll have a double load? I deserve a raise but maybe this is a bad time to ask because we lost a big contract. But then, is there ever a good time? The boss is always in a rotten mood lately. So what are you going to do? Make up your mind... Decide!

There is this great bargain of a boat. The fellow down the road has bought a bigger one and he wants to get rid of the old one, which is just right for the two of you. But you did promise the wife that economy trip to Europe for your anniversary. Nine countries in two weeks! You can't beat that. So which one is it... boat or Europe? Or can you have both?

How about that mink coat? A one day special... $6,000 reduced to $3,500... a steal! But you just renewed your $10,000 C.D., and that's all the savings you have. There's not enough in the checking account. You don't want to take out the C.D., lose the interest and pay a penalty. But you still want the coat. There must be a way to get it. Is there?

The FIVE-MINUTE PROBLEM SOLVER will help you find possibilities you might not have recognized, and guide you into making the right decisions from the best choices available.

Depending on your life and work experience, what may be a simple problem to one person might be a monumental hurdle to another. Take the case of someone having to assemble an exercycle or piece of furniture from parts according to printed instructions... You have to fit Part A into Part D, while you hold Parts B and C together between your legs, as you balance Part E on your head in preparation for topping the whole thing by putting finishing screws into designated holes, two of which don't seem to fit at all...

Only a person experienced in assembling things might find this job easy. But if you are less handy, the instructions translated from a foreign language, and written with an accent, might make it an enormously difficult task.

So, perhaps making a decision to buy fully assembled pieces, even though more expensive, instead of unassembled ones which are cheaper but more of a problem, might be wise. Or are there still other options?

Find out from the FIVE-MINUTE PROBLEM SOLVER. The nine simple steps described in this book will lead you into formulating creative ideas, spur you into logical action, and keep you from wasting valuable time and energy on non-productive choices. From the first step to the last, you follow a logical sequence of ideas straight to your goal or decision.

So, what is the FIVE-MINUTE PROBLEM SOLVER and what are the nine steps?

NO REASON TO BE IN DOUBT,
  FIND OUT WHAT IT'S ALL ABOUT.
ALL YOU DO IS SIMPLIFY,
  IT ISN'T HARD... GO AHEAD AND TRY.

First, DEAL With the Problem

It's hard not to react when your comfort and security are being threatened, and problems can do that. You look for ways to deal with them, but unless you know what your are doing, you may get yourself into even deeper trouble. So, begin to do it the correct way...

Start by defining the problem. Spell it out, break it down into simple terms. Sometimes there are so many different aspects to a problem that it may be difficult to pinpoint the exact situation which created the problem in the first place.

So, first we "DEAL" with the problem by determining the "KEY THOUGHT." By that I mean whatever occurred or exists that caused the problem in the first place.

Here are a couple of simple examples:

"What can I do about the bills piling up at the end of the month? Should I pay a few and let the others slide, or take out a loan, pay the whole bunch off and consolidate my payments over six months or more?"

The "KEY THOUGHT" here is, "I don't have enough money to pay all my bills at the end of the month." There would be no problem if you did, would there?

Another:

"My boss and I just don't see eye to eye. He wants me to work on a program that I honestly feel is ridiculous and will result in complete disaster... and I'll get the blame, of course! He's definitely not the type to take criticism, and he's got a rotten temper...

"Should I tell him what I think and risk being fired, or try to do the best I can with his crazy request?"

The "KEY THOUGHT" is: "My boss gave me this assignment that I feel will lead me into complete disaster." If he hadn't there would be no problem, right?

The first step, then, is to "DEAL" with the problem.

"DEAL" stands for:

(D), *Define* the exact problem by determining the "KEY THOUGHT."

(E), *Elucidate,* or clarify the problem, so that you can begin to...

(A), *Act* on it... You know what your problem is, and once armed with this knowledge, you can...

(L), *Lead* into the next step, to "COPE," which shows what choices you have and, believe me, there are usually more than you thought of when you first faced the situation.

The next chapter will show you how to "COPE" with your problem.

YOU HAVE MORE CHOICES
  THAN YOU THINK.
THIS GAME IS NOT PLAYED
  IN A WINK.
SO CHECK OUT EVERY MOVE TWICE
  BEFORE YOU FINALLY ROLL THE DICE.

Second, "COPE" With the Problem

Decision making is easy when there is an obvious choice. For example, you go to the store to get some soft ice cream on a nasty, stormy night. The only two flavors available are vanilla and chocolate. Your favorite is vanilla, but the vanilla machine is broken. The decision, therefore, is already made for you. You take chocolate or nothing. Of course, you could choose another option. You could drive a couple of miles further in stormy weather to another store that, hopefully, would have a vanilla machine working. If you are a chocoholic, however, you were in luck at your first store. You didn't have to make a decision about moving on. In fact, you didn't even have a problem!

The alternative option, then, depends on your motivation. If your happiness that evening depended on getting soft, vanilla ice cream, you would have gone on to the next store regardless of the weather. If it weren't that important, you would have settled for chocolate or forgotten the whole thing. Your problem was a very personal one, the "KEY THOUGHT" being that the machine making vanilla ice cream was broken down.

Now, suppose your wife is pregnant and craves soft, vanilla ice cream. It's raining cats and dogs, but you venture forth like Galahad to the local ice cream store wrapped tightly in a heavy-duty rubberized coat. But, of course, the soft, vanilla ice cream machine is out of order. Do you go home empty-handed and hope the wife will be content to munch on a pickle, or do you drive to the next store a few miles down the road, a road with a nasty reputation for flooding? Now you have a problem and a decision to make...

Now, what is the "KEY THOUGHT" in this situation? Can you find it? Is it the same as in the first problem... that the machine making vanilla ice cream is broken down?

Not really... In this case the "KEY THOUGHT" is that your *pregnant wife* craves soft, vanilla ice cream. The fact that the vanilla ice cream machine is broken is a secondary matter. This is no longer a personal problem based only on what is needed for your own happiness. You just don't know how your pregnant wife is going to take the news that she can't have soft, vanilla ice cream tonight... and will she or won't she be satisfied munching on a pickle instead? You have to decide which alternative you'd rather face... an upset, pregnant wife, or a couple of miles of possibly flooded road.

Now that we've determined the "KEY THOUGHT," and defined the exact problem, we can begin to "COPE" with the situation. In other words, try to resolve the soft, vanilla ice cream dilemma.

"COPE" stands for:

(C), *Choices*... List all alternatives that come to mind.

(O), *Opportunities*... that may make the solution easier.

(P), *Possibilities*... that you might otherwise have overlooked.

(E), *Effects*... that should be considered, so that the solution to one problem doesn't create another.

After you have listed all the choices you can think of, go ahead and check them out. The next chapter on "ADD" will show you how to do this more thoroughly, but meanwhile just think about them as calmly and objectively as possible... In doing this you will probably discover other possibilities and opportunities that you hadn't thought of before.

O.K., let's "COPE" with the problem at hand...

First, how many *choices* are there in the case of the pregnant wife who craves soft, vanilla ice cream?

Well, three choices are obvious: (1) Buy nothing, and hope she'll be satisfied munching a pickle... (2) Buy chocolate, and hope she won't get too upset that it's not vanilla... or (3) Phone ahead and make certain the next store has the vanilla machine in working order. If they do, drive to that location, but be certain to bring your water wings just in case.

At this point it's a good idea to sit down for a few minutes and think about these choices, and see if any other *opportunities* or *possibilities* come to mind.

Here's one... How about phoning your wife and explaining the situation to her? She may be very rational about the whole thing and tell you to forget it and just come home safely. Or, if they're easily available, flowers accompanying the chocolate ice cream might just do the trick.

Now let's look back at the other two problems we mentioned in the chapter on "DEAL." First, the one where the bills remain unpaid at the end of the month. We've already determined the "KEY THOUGHT" here... "I don't have enough money to pay all my bills at the end of the month."

Let's review the *choices* available so far: (1) I can pay a few and let the others slide, or (2) take out a bill-payer loan to pay them all and consolidate my payments over six months or more...

Are there any other options? Think about it... maybe there are other opportunities and possibilities available, but always consider the effects... We don't want to create more problems than we already have.

Now, let's look at the problem of your boss's crazy assignment. Remember the "KEY THOUGHT" here? "My boss gave me this assignment that will lead me into a complete disaster!"

If we consider *choices,* we can come up with three right away... (1) Have a head-on talk with your boss. Get him in a good mood, if possible, and try to be diplomatic and persuasive. Maybe you can talk him out of his crazy idea, or perhaps help him talk himself out of it. Just don't make him look, or feel like a fool. If he does that himself... that's his problem. (2) If you don't think you are up to it, perhaps you can talk an associate of yours into requesting the assignment. Tell him why you think he's a much better choice for this deal, and how he can really profit from it. It's just not up your alley, or you don't really have the time to do the assignment justice. It's important to remember, however, that your associate isn't overly concerned with *your* problems. You had better think carefully about benefits to him if he takes on the challenge. (3) If your associate agrees, take him with you when you talk to your boss about the assignment, and explain how changing roles will benefit the company. But you better be prepared with some iron-clad suggestions which will sound reasonable to him...

In the next chapter we'll "ADD" up these choices. We'll check them out thoroughly and determine which one has the most potential to solve your problem.

SOME THINGS ARE GOOD,
  SOME ARE BAD.
IT'S A GOOD IDEA TO CHECK
  WHICH YOU'VE HAD.
SAVE THE BEST,
  DISCARD WHAT YOU DON'T NEED.
PLANT A NEW FLOWER,
  PLUCK OUT THE WEED.

Third, "ADD" Up Your Choices

Suppose we get back to the broken soft, vanilla ice cream machine. So far we've been able to "DEAL" with the problem by defining the "KEY THOUGHT," namely that your pregnant wife wants soft, vanilla ice cream. Then we've "COPE"'d with the situation by listing several CHOICES, OPPORTUNITIES and POSSIBILITIES that might help solve the problem. Now we're going to "ADD" up these choices, insofar as their ADVANTAGES, DISADVANTAGES and DEVELOPMENT OF NEW IDEAS are concerned, so that we can determine which may be the best course of action to take.

"ADD," therefore stands for:

(A), *ADVANTAGES*. . . Make a list for each choice.

(D), *DISADVANTAGES*. . . Make a list for each choice.

(D), *DEVELOP NEW IDEAS*. . . These can be in any size, shape or dimension. Let your imagination loose on this one and strike out in new directions. You may be pleasantly surprised to find what happens.

Remember our first choice? It was, "buy nothing and hope your pregnant wife will be satisfied with munching a pickle."

Are there any ADVANTAGES to this choice? Can you think of any? Well, here are a couple of possibilities. . .

(1) Munching a pickle, or maybe promising her a diamond bracelet, might just take her mind off ice cream completely.

(2) Perhaps she'd appreciate being told the facts and deciding for herself whether or not she can do without the ice cream.

What are the DISADVANTAGES? Any ideas? How about these. . .

(1) Bringing home nothing at all might be the biggest gamble you could make. Who knows how she will react?

(2) Then again, she might not be interested in munching a pickle. Maybe Sushi might be her next request, and if the Japanese take-outs are closed you might have to take a quick flight to Japan.

The second choice, if you recall, was, "Buy chocolate ice cream and hope she won't get too upset that it's not vanilla."

One ADVANTAGE to this choice is that you're not coming

home empty-handed. At least you brought back some soft ice cream.

Another is if she doesn't want it, you'll have yourself a treat. After all, isn't chocolate an aphrodisiac? Or have you had enough of that already?

Of course, a possible DISADVANTAGE to bringing home a substitute flavor is that, if her mood is unreceptive, you might irritate her even more. And that you certainly don't need.

The third choice was to call ahead to the next soft ice cream store and make certain whether or not they have vanilla available. The ADVANTAGE here is that you're not wasting your time traveling in the rain on a wild goose chase; and secondly, if they happen to have soft vanilla ice cream, then that automatically solves your problem. A DISADVANTAGE, however, might be the distance to be traveled in such nasty weather and, also, keeping your wife waiting so much longer for her favorite flavor might not improve her mood at all.

Now that you've listed all the ADVANTAGES and DIS-ADVANTAGES of each choice, how about trying to DEVELOP NEW IDEAS? The most obvious would be to phone your pregnant wife to discuss the choices with her, instead of running back and forth on such a nasty night. At least, if nothing else, you'll find out if she's in a reasonable or a "you'd better, or else," mood. Armed with that knowledge you can proceed with appropriate action.

Another NEW IDEA might be to try your powers of persuasion. While you have her on the phone, why not try to talk her into becoming a chocoholic? After all, vanilla is pretty plain. Chocolate is more colorful and certainly has a richer, more robust flavor. Lay it on in a convincing manner and you may be able to convert her.

Now let's apply "ADD" to the other two problems mentioned in Chapter One.

The KEY THOUGHT of the first was, "I don't have enough money to pay all my bills at the end of the month."

Choice #1 was: "Pay a few and let the others slide..." What are the ADVANTAGES? Well, at least the creditors you pay will be happy with you; but then, of course, the DISADVANTAGES are, (1) those you don't pay may start collection procedures against you, and (2) your credit rating will not be helped.

Choice #2 was: "Take out a bill-payer loan from the bank and settle with the whole bunch immediately, while consolidating payments over a convenient time span..."

ADVANTAGES are, (1) all your creditors will be satisfied, (2) consolidating payments usually reduces interest charges, and (3) your credit rating will not be endangered.

The DISADVANTAGE, however, is that you are obligating yourself to a fairly large series of monthly payments that you better be certain you can manage. Another DISADVANTAGE is that you will have to discipline your spending habits and go on a strict budget. You won't be able to add any new debts to your long list of obligations until you've paid off the old ones.

Now that you've considered the "A" and "D," the ADVANTAGES and DISADVANTAGES of these choices and their probable effects, can you "D," DEVELOP any new ideas, opportunities or possibilities that might help to solve your problem?

Here's one idea... contact your creditors, explain your situation and request a pay out or a more extended installment arrangement. Creditors may be sympathetic to your plight, especially if you assure them you're going on a strict budget. This choice will eliminate most of the DISADVANTAGES of the other choices we've discussed.

Can you think of any other new ideas? Well, here's a possibility. If you're lucky enough to have one available, tap a rich aunt or uncle for a quick loan. Tell them you need your inheritance now. Of course, you're assuming they intended to mention you in their wills, but even if they weren't, this might be an effective hint. And if you can swing a deal like this, you'll solve your problem promptly. Unless your relative is very friendly indeed, however, he, or she, will expect you to pay the loan back. So it's up to you to try for the most convenient terms possible.

The point is, by "ADD"ing up the choices, you've come up with something of value. In other words, it's made you think about all the opportunities and possibilities available to you. Now you can determine which choice has the greatest number of advantages, and which the least, and this, of course, can help you solve your problem more effectively.

Remember the KEY THOUGHT of the other problem we discussed? It was... "My boss gave me this assignment that will lead me into complete disaster!"

Let's "ADD" up the choices previously mentioned...

The first was: "Face your boss eye to eye and try to talk him out of his impossible idea." One ADVANTAGE already discussed is that (1) He might talk himself out of it with a little help from you. Perhaps you can very diplomatically steer him into realizing he could wind up in quicksand if he carried out his plan. It would help if this turned out to be his conclusion, not yours. Admittedly, this could be very tricky.

(2) Another ADVANTAGE is that the way you present the picture to your boss, with a possible solution, could give him a better impression of you. He may finally discover that you are a thinker, an executive with imagination and the guts to carry an idea through to a successful conclusion.

One DISADVANTAGE, of course, is that, (1) if not handled properly, your boss might not be able to save face, and would look the fool he is... So out comes the guillotine and your head may roll. (2) Another may be that if he's insecure in any way, questioning his authority in this matter might bring out his resentment. So this may just have to be a calculated risk on your part.

Now that you've been able to "ADD" and evaluate the choices available to solve your problem, the next chapter will help you "OWN" up to your responsibility to others' wishes and needs.

CHECK THE NEEDS OF OTHERS
TO ACCOMPLISH YOUR GOAL.
SHARING WITH OTHERS
IS GOOD FOR YOUR SOUL.

Fourth, "OWN" Up to Others' Wishes and Needs

Since the problem and its solution often involve other people beside yourself, it may be very important to get their points of view before proceeding any further with your preferred choice of action.

Step Four in the "FIVE-MINUTE PROBLEM SOLVER" therefore is "OWN," which stands for... *Others' Wishes and Needs.*

In the example of the pregnant wife who craves soft vanilla ice cream, of course, the husband must "OWN" up to her wishes and needs or he'll hear about it when he's a great-grandfather. The entire problem rests on her wish and supposed need for that particular type and flavor ice cream. So, as we've mentioned before, this is the "KEY THOUGHT," right here. In this example, then, Step Four must be handled from the very start. But consider it again at this point because you should begin thinking about alternatives and other options available to you now... Such as, "Does she even like pickles at all?" and, "If I drove to the next ice cream store, would she mind being left alone for an extra hour or so?" These are all things to take into account when "OWN"ing up to the wife's wishes and needs.

Regarding the problem in which the "KEY THOUGHT" is,... "I don't have enough money to pay all my bills at the end of the month," you must also "OWN" up to others' wishes and needs. Specifically, (1) your spouse, if any, (2) your creditors, of course, (3) your banker, if you apply for a loan, or (4) your rich relative if he (or she) will part with some cash to help you out.

In fact, if you carefully "OWN" up to all these people's wishes and needs, you may be able to determine the best way to approach them in this matter. After all, you wouldn't want to step on anyone's toes. In fact, you'll discover which option offers the best chance for getting out of hock most efficiently.

The case of your difficult boss requires extra careful "OWN"ing up to others' wishes and needs. In the first place, you certainly don't want to irritate the guy in charge. That's a no-no! Then again he wants you to carry out his crazy scheme and he needs you to do it without griping. But since you intend to gripe anyway, do it with aplombe and great discretion so as not to make him lose face or look like a fool . . . granted, not an easy task!

So, as you consider others' wishes and needs, you gain important insight into how your spouse, family and associates will respond to your choice. This will help you formulate your plan of action with a better than even chance to get what you want.

In the next chapter, Step Five in the ''FIVE-MINUTE PRO-BLEM SOLVER,'' we will begin to ''WIN,'' or determine *What Is Needed* to solve your problem effectively.

To make the FIVE-MINUTE PROBLEM SOLVER work for you:

1. DEAL with the problem. Define the Key Thought, without which there would be no problem at all.

2. COPE with the problem. List all possible choices. Just make sure your choice won't get you into any unnecessary trouble.

3. ADD up the problem. Write down all the advantages and dis advantages for each choice. Then think of some new ideas, if possible, even if they might be way out. Carefully evaluate all this information to determine your best course of action. This decision is based on whichever choice has the most advantages and the least number of disadvantages.

4. OWN up to others' wishes and needs. Consider your family's and other's responses to your choice of action, and how this may affect your final decision.

YOU'VE DONE ALL TO PREPARE
  FOR YOUR MOVE WITH CARE.
THE TIME HAS COME TO START THE ACTION.
  FOLLOW THROUGH WITHOUT DISTRACTION.

Fifth, Begin to "WIN"

You can relax now,. . . the hard part's over. You've arrived at the half-way point.

The Five-Minute Problem Solver has shown you how to "DEAL" with your problem, how to "COPE," "ADD," and "OWN" up to others' wishes and needs.

Now you will begin to "WIN" the solution to your problem.

"WIN" stands for *What Is Needed.* It helps you decide what steps, materials and procedures are required to achieve the solution.

O.K., WHAT IS NEEDED to solve the problem of the pregnant wife who craves soft, vanilla ice cream during a nasty rainstorm?

Well, after having "ADD"ed up the ADVANTAGES, DISADVANTAGES and DEVELOPED New Ideas and determined the best choice of action, let's say you've decided it would be smart to bring home soft, vanilla ice cream instead of a substitute.

"WHAT IS NEEDED?" In other words, what do you do first?

(1) Well, you've already developed the new idea that you should phone home before you go anywhere else. (2) Make sure the wife knows all the facts: a). the soft, vanilla ice cream machine is broken down in the store you went to, and b). it's a very nasty, rainy night and the next store is at least ½ hour drive away. (3) Her reaction to your tale of woe will decide your next step. She'll no doubt make it very clear whether or not she wants soft, vanilla ice cream under these circumstances. Either she won't blink an eyelash at your having to drive an extra hour round-trip, or she'll relent and forget the whole thing. Whatever her maneuver, you'll know "WHAT IS NEEDED" to figure out your next move. Happy checkmate!

Let's go back to the second problem of not having enough money to pay all the bills at the end of the month.

If you've "ADD"ed up your choices and decided the best course of action is to apply for a bill-payer loan from your local bank, and then stick to a stricter budget, WHAT IS NEEDED to start the ball rolling?

Well, first you'll have to select a bank to process your loan application. It would seem logical to choose the bank where you keep your savings and checking accounts.

Second, collect your charge account records, bank account numbers and prepare a financial statement showing your assets and liabilities. These will expedite your application and give the loan officer a better impression of your ability to repay the loan on time. And don't wear your jogging suit and track shoes when you go to see him. He wants to make sure you stay put long enough to repay the loan.

How about that third problem we've been considering... The one where your boss insists on that assignment which you feel may wreck your entire career. WHAT IS NEEDED in this case?

If you've done your "ADD"ing up and decided to try talking the old boy into seeing the light, you'd better (1) work up a complete statement and background presentation to show him why your suggestion has merit. If he buys that, (2) have a thorough proposal prepared to demonstrate how that favorite project of yours could be of much greater value to the company, and how it has a better chance for success; most of all, how it will reflect his good judgment and earn him great prestige.

In this way, your boss can save face and light up yours, hopefully with a raise or promotion.

Step 6 in the FIVE-MINUTE PROBLEM SOLVER will "SET" the final Sequence, Expense and Time required to achieve your goal.

IT'S TIME YOU FIND OUT
   WHAT'S AT STAKE;
HOW MUCH TIME AND MONEY
   IT'LL TAKE.

WHAT DO YOU DO FIRST
   TO GET IT GOING,
SO THAT YOU CAN MAKE
   YOUR VERY BEST SHOWING?

.

Sixth, Get "SET" for Action

Congratulations! You've made it. The Five-Minute Problem Solver has now brought you to the point where you're ready to solve your problem, hopefully without sprouting any gray hairs.

As we've seen in Step Five, "WIN" determines the materials and requirements necessary for the solution. The next step "SET"'s the stage for action by listing the necessary procedures in correct order.

"SET" stands for: *Sequence, Expense and Time,* and considers what has to be done, how much it will cost and how much time it will take to accomplish. It's important to get pencil and paper and start writing it all down, because this is the recipe for the successful attainment of your goals.

Now, in the case of the pregnant wife who craves soft, vanilla ice cream on a miserably rainy night, it would be a miracle if the husband remembers to take his wallet with him to pay for the ice cream, let alone remember to take pencil and paper along to jot down ideas. Yet, if he had practiced this method of problem-solving, he would know how to figure out the steps quickly. Of course, there is the little wallet-size Five-Minute Problem Solver which can be detached at the end of this book, which he can carry next to his heart or his driver's license. But if he is a novice at this technique it would be wise to whip out the pencil and paper, find a convenient countertop, wall or someone's back and make written notes for the plan of action. This will provide him with the guidelines necessary to solve his problem.

The basis for SEQUENCE has already been outlined in the last chapter. Remember? First, you're going to phone home... Second, you'll discuss the entire situation with your pregnant wife... Third, depending on her reaction, you'll decide whether: (a) to forget the whole thing and go home empty-handed, but safe and sound, (b) bring home a substitute, like chocolate, or (c) phone ahead and go on to the next store that has soft, vanilla ice cream.

SEQUENCE, then, covers all angles adequately and logically while clarifying the available options and alternatives. Isn't it better to know where you're going beforehand, rather than kicking yourself afterwards when everything's gone wrong? That's the purpose of SEQUENCE... to help you pre-plan your moves effectively before you go into action, and perhaps saving you from headaches later on.

As far as EXPENSE is concerned, the cost of the soft, vanilla ice cream, a phone call home and possibly extra gas for the drive to the next ice cream store is not likely to break the bank. But just for the record, jot it all down. The technique may prove very helpful in other instances. So get into a good habit.

The additional TIME required for all this procrastination, however, may cause some marital strain, depending on the pregnant wife's mood. When you phone home, therefore, be sure to remind her that you'll be home much faster if she doesn't object to a substitute for soft, vanilla ice cream.

Now, get "SET" for the second problem we've been considering... not having enough money to pay all the bills at the end of the month. Again, the "SEQUENCE" has been outlined in the last chapter ("WIN"), but write it down on paper at this time for reinforcement.

Recall what is needed? First, choose your bank. Second, collect your credit record statements. Third, prepare a financial statement. Fourth, make application for a bill-payer loan.

The "TIME" needed to achieve your goal includes... (1) the time necessary to collect your records and apply for the loan, and (2) the time it takes for the bank to, hopefully, approve your loan. Both of these steps together should usually take no more than a few days.

As far as "EXPENSE" is concerned, there are usually no costs involved in these procedures... so, fortunately, this part of "SET" is not applicable.

Now, let's get "SET" for the third problem... the one where your boss presents you with an assignment that may ruin your career.

Begin with writing down the "SEQUENCE" in correct order... Remember your plan of action involves trying to talk him out of the assignment altogether.

Again working from your listing of "What is Needed" the "SEQUENCE" required might include the following...

(1) Prepare a background presentation detailing your counter-proposal. (2) Draw up a list of reasons showing your boss why your ideas will work. (3) Emphasize the positive aspects of your suggestions and justify your position. Don't even mention the negative aspects of your boss's program. (4) Show him how your proposal, when implemented, will bring success and prestige to both the company and him personally.

If all this seems like a tall order, don't fret. Having followed the previous steps of the Five-Minute Problem Solver to the letter will prepare you well enough to win half the battle even before you meet with your boss.

"EXPENSE" is again not applicable in this instance, but the "TIME" involved includes your research and writing up the notes for "SEQUENCE" presentation outlined above. Since you can't afford to let any grass grow under your feet, set a time limit to work this out and do a thorough job. Speed is of the essence . . . So get busy!

Now we're ready for the next step, so let's "GO."

KEEP IN MIND
JUST WHERE YOU'RE GOING,
THERE COULD BE SETBACKS
WITHOUT YOUR KNOWING.
KEEP A SHARP LOOKOUT FOR THOSE,
BEFORE YOU STEP ON ANY TOES.

Seventh, "GO"

Now that you've determined "What Is Needed," and you're "SET" for action, let's "GO" for it.

"GO" stands for *Goals and Obstacles,* or (1) what it is you want to happen, and (2) what situations may come up that can stand in the way of solving your problem.

Take the pregnant wife, if you will... What is the goal in this case? What are the possible obstacles?

Well, if you're the husband, you'd want to make your pregnant wife happy... What will make her happy? Soft, vanilla ice cream at this moment. Now, remember, you haven't seen her for a half hour or more... Her craving may be gone by now. But since your goal is to make her happy, while, at the same time, avoid drowning in the downpour, a phone call home first to discuss the whole problem with her would seem a logical next move on your part.

Are there any obstacles that might arise? You bet there are! First of all, you can't depend on your wife making things easier for you. Why should she? She's the one with cravings, morning sickness and the shape of a blimp. So, you might as well anticipate the worst... But then again, maybe you married a saint who'll agree with your solution to bring home a substitute...

Treat all obstacles that might arise as opportunities to reconsider and modify your course of action in the best way possible. Make your wife happy. If she insists on soft, vanilla ice cream tonight... so be it! She'll just have to be a little patient, until you get your passport in order.

Now, let's "GO" to the second problem we've been considering... the one about lack of finances to cover the monthly expenses.

What's the goal? Simply, to arrange for enough money to pay all the bills at the end of the month.

Are there obstacles? Of course there are. Any situation that might prevent or impede your obtaining a bank loan is a real biggie. For instance, a poor credit rating, excessive outstanding loans and/or credit accounts, an unimpressive employment record, etc.

Be aware of these possible stumbling blocks and either try to clear your record, if necessary, before applying for a loan, or be prepared to explain how you are improving your financial situation by working with a budget consultant or advisor of some sort.

What is your goal in our third problem?... the one where your boss gives you that disastrous assignment? It is, of course, to get him to change his mind... Either to eliminate it altogether, assign it to someone else or to change it to something you feel you can handle successfully.

What are the obstacles? Your boss is the main one... Without him there would be no problem, right?

Any others? Well, his reaction to your proposal may be unfavorable, or he may remain adamant just to remind you who's the boss.

Again, bear these possible obstacles in mind so that you won't be taken by surprise if they present themselves. In fact, try to think of one or two things you might say or do to ward off the onslaught. Who knows? You could still pull a rabbit out of the hat or at least save face.

The next step in the Five-Minute Problem Solver, number eight, will ''WRAP'' it up and finalize your decision.

YOU'VE CHECKED IT ALL OUT,
THERE'S NO MORE DOUBT.
IT'S TIME TO PROCEED...
AHEAD WITH FULL SPEED.

Eighth, "WRAP" It Up

The previous step, "GO," considered your goals and alerted you to any obstacles you might encounter along the way.

Now you are prepared to "WRAP" it up...

"WRAP" stands for:

(W) *Work* towards a final decision... no turning back now.

(R) *Reinforce* this decision in your own mind by quickly reviewing the steps that led up to it,

(A) *And*...

(P) Now, *Proceed* to act on it!

The time for contemplation and doubts is over... give yourself permission to get on with it.

How would you "WRAP" up the case of the pregnant wife?

Well, by now you've very carefully considered all the angles in the previous seven steps. Now get to WORK... Phone home and discuss the alternatives with your wife.

REINFORCE your decision by recalling the various options you've considered through steps 1 through 7, and the reasons you chose this particular one. You've thought the problem through, including your goals and possible obstacles, and are hoping for the best but prepared for the worst.

Finally, PROCEED to act on your choice... Get out that coin or telephone credit card, if you have one, and call home.

What about "WRAP"ping up our second problem... insufficient finances to pay the bills at the end of the month. Remember?... You decided the best option open to you was to apply for a loan from your local bank.

What's the best way to "WRAP" it up?

First, WORK to finalize your decision. Ask yourself... was there any other option available to you that might work out better? Not really. Since you can't let the problem just slide and you don't have a rich relative to tap for a quick interest-free loan. So, yours is the best decision after all.

REINFORCE this choice by briefly reviewing the steps that brought you to it. Then, PROCEED with your course of action. Go over WHAT IS NEEDED, get SET and GO.

How do you "WRAP" up the problem of your boss's crazy assignment? Remember, if possible you're going to try to talk him out of it altogether. This is your goal. Should this approach fail, you still have two other options, as discussed in the previous chapter.

WORK to finalize your decision and prepare to back up your arguments. Then REINFORCE by reviewing the mental processes that resulted in this choice... Steps 1 through 7 of the Five-Minute Problem Solver, and finally PROCEED to act on it.

Arrange for an appointment with your boss to discuss your ideas, keep all your facts in order and use the big guns... your crystal-clear and persuasive proposals that will show your boss how much you really care for his and the company's well-being, in a very positive way, of course.

Now that you've "WRAP"ped up your plan of action, we come to the final step... to "SECURE" your decision by formulating it concisely in your mind.

How do you do that?

SIT BACK AND SMILE,
  YOU'VE WORKED HARD FOR A WHILE.
YOU'VE BURST THE BUBBLE,
  TAKEN CARE OF YOUR TROUBLE.
NO MORE STRESS...
  ENJOY YOUR SUCCESS.

Ninth, "Secure" Your Goal

The final step in the Five-Minute Problem Solver will show you how to achieve the mental and physical relaxation necessary to focus your mind on successfully solving your problem. It then helps you support your action right up to the complete solution to the problem.

"SECURE" stands for:

(S), *Support* the thought of winning.

(E), *End* all doubts.

(C), *Complete* the process of relaxation.

(U), *Uphold* the image.

(R), *Reward* yourself for a job well done, and . . . Keep up your

(E), *Enthusiasm.*

Let's get back to the problem of the pregnant wife who craves soft, vanilla ice cream on a nasty night. You've worked through the problem using the first eight steps of the FIVE-MINUTE PROBLEM SOLVER, and decided the best choice of action is to phone home from the shop with the broken vanilla ice cream machine, discussing the whole situation with the wife and either talking her out of her obsession or, failing that, working out the most sensible alternative.

But first, take a few minutes and think of something else, something pleasant that will relax you and clear away all the tension left over from thinking so hard about your problem . . . Take a few deep breaths and calmly review your decision. This will help you SUPPORT the thought of winning. No more deliberation . . . You can now END all doubts, and you're ready to COMPLETE the process of relaxation while you follow through on your plan of action. UPHOLD an image of success in your mind, and REWARD yourself for a job well done. How about a special flavor of ice cream for yourself? No? Well, at least congratulate yourself for having seen this problem through.

Keep up your ENTHUSIASM for your success as you phone the wife and solve the mystery . . . Will she or will she not take another flavor instead of vanilla? Regardless, you have come this far and you'll see it through. You know you can do it! You now have that special knack for solving problems... Go to it.

Similarly, regarding the problem of insufficient funds to pay your bills at the end of the month, as well as the one where your boss has given you that disastrous assignment... SECURE your goal by following the steps of the FIVE-MINUTE PROBLEM SOLVER, then relax for a few minutes to get the cobwebs cleared from your mind and take a few deep breaths... SUPPORT the thought of winning, END all doubts, COMPLETE the process by UPHOLDing the image of success, REWARD yourself for a job well done, and keep up your ENTHUSIASM as you carry out your choice of action successfully.

In practical terms, once you've learned to use this technique, the whole procedure can take a minute. If you have some time to spare for complete relaxation, however,...

Close your eyes, breathe deeply a few times while you slowly count from ten to one, and let yourself go mentally to that pleasant place where you've enjoyed yourself in the past... Then eliminate all extraneous thoughts and focus on the steps leading up to your final choice of action. Then just visualize success... SECURE your goal and SUPPORT your decision. By now, you can erase all the doubts and be ready to concentrate on the solution to the problem.

To summarize the FIVE-MINUTE PROBLEM SOLVER so that you can easily make it work for you in five-minutes:

1. Steps (1), (2) and (3) define the problem (DEAL), evaluate choices (COPE) and determine the best possible solution (ADD).
2. Steps (4) through (8) consider the merits of the choice in regard to what others may think of it (OWN), what is needed to achieve it (WIN), what has to be done first, how long it will take to accomplish, and how much it will cost (SET). The choice is then finalized by determining your goal (what you really want to happen), what obstacles may be encountered and what can be done to remove them (GO).
3. Finally, if you decide to go ahead with your choice of action, Step (8) shows you how to keep your mind focused on achieving that goal by working at it (WRAP), and Step (9) helps you accomplish your goal and solve your problem (SECURE).

Let's Solve Some Problems

When you first look at a problem, it may seem that only an ''either - or'' solution is possible... For example,

''Should I go west with my company or stay here with my family and look for a new job?''

It's one way or the other; but is it really?

Or, ''Shall I buy the new fur coat, or put my money in the bank?''

Here again, it's either one or the other... Right?

Not necessarily. The Five-Minute Problem Solver will show you other possible solutions, and pinpoint one which probably best solves your dilemma.

For example, here's a problem my friend Jane presented to me one morning over coffee...

''I have $10,000 which I'd like to invest,'' she told me, ''but my home needs repairs costing just about that amount. What shall I do?''

''Well,'' I began thoughtfully, ''first, let's DEAL with the problem...''

DEAL

''Let's begin by defining it exactly. The whole thing seems to boil down to not having enough money to both invest and repair your home at the same time.''

''Correct,'' Jane answered.

''This is the Key Thought... without which there would be no problem,'' I continued.

''Great!'' she smiled, ''Now, where do I go from here?''

You COPE,'' I replied...

COPE

''How? By listing all the Choices, Opportunities, Possibilities and Effects that come to mind... At first glance I already see the two obvious choices: either invest the $10,000 or use the money to repair your home. It's either one way or the other. Right?''

48

"That's the way it looks to me," admitted Jane.

"Let's think about it," I said. "Are there any other possibilities?"

"Maybe... I could get some financial help from another source."

"Such as?"

"Well, I might be able to get a second mortgage..., or I could sell my home altogether."

"You see?" I commented, "you're already coming up with good new ideas."

"In fact, I can think of a couple of other way-out possibilities," she continued. "I might borrow $10,000 as an interest-free loan from my Aunt Marge... she's loaded! But forget it... she's a tightwad."

"What's the other possibility?" I asked.

"I could sell my grandmother's brooch... It must be worth $10,000 by this time," she replied.

"Well, that might be something to think about. But first," I continued, refilling her cup, "let's ADD up each of the choices we feel are most useful."

ADD

"The first one was to invest the $10,000... What are the Advantages of this choice?"

"Well," Jane mused, "it should earn interest or dividends, for one thing. For another, the investment funds can be made available in case of emergencies."

"How would that make you feel?"

"Well, I'd feel financially secure."

"That sounds good... How about the Disadvantages to this choice?"

"Obviously there are no funds available for immediate home repairs, which, unfortunately, are badly needed," Jane replied. "Also, the house will deteriorate and lose value... and repair costs will probably go up in the future. Besides, I don't like living with the feeling that the house may cave in on me at any time... But, then again, if I invest and lose my investment, I might lose the house, too..."

49

"So we'll rule that out," I noted. How about looking at it from a different angle... What can you do with the house as it is to make more money? Can we Develop some New Ideas on this choice?"

"That is a new angle... Well, let me think," mused Jane. "I guess I could rent out an extra room, or perhaps use one room as a tax deduction for business purposes... But what business?"

"Doesn't your husband, Jack, do a lot of work at home?"

"I see what you're getting at," Jane smiled knowingly... Jack can claim his home work space as a tax deduction."

"Ask him to check with his accountant for the details," I nodded in agreement, "just to make sure it's feasible in his case."

"Now, let's go to Choice number two... to repair your home with the $10,000. What are the Advantages?"

"Well, for one," replied Jane, "my home would certainly be safer. It would also probably increase in value, be more comfortable to live in, and may even improve our health by eliminating hazards. Things are always breaking down now... We already have two broken steps on the stairwell."

"Are there any Disadvantages to using the money for repairs?"

"Sure," she said, "I'd have no funds left for investment or for any financial emergencies which might arise at any moment. Besides, investment earnings that could add to future income just wouldn't be there... That doesn't exactly make me feel secure."

"Well, then," I said, "How about Developing some New Ideas?"

"I can't think of any."

"Maybe repairs can be done gradually instead of all at one time, which would eat up your $10,000... And if you and Jack could do some of the repairs yourselves with used or rebuilt parts, you might be able to save a lot of money."

"That's possible," she agreed. "I don't know, though... Jack is such a klutz. But," her face brightened, "my neighbor across the street, he's really handy, and real good-looking... what muscles..."

"Uh-huh, I bet," I said. "Let's get back to Choice number three... selling your home altogether. What are the Advantages to that one?''

"Well, it would take care of all my repair problems for one thing... And maybe we could take the money we get for the house and use it for a down payment on a new property."

"That sounds good, Jane," I said. "Are there any Disadvantages to this choice?"

"There certainly is one! I'll have to look for a new home immediately, and, in today's inflated market, that might be pretty difficult to do. With the money I'll get I might only be able to exchange one headache for another."

"Can you think of any New Ideas in this regard?" I asked. Jane shook her head.

"What if you sold your home and rented an apartment for a while... Would this save you money?"

"I don't think so. Rents are so high these days... it would probably be about the same as mortgage payments in my area."

"Then consider a new neighborhood, perhaps further out in the suburbs where apartment rents might be cheaper. Then again, you might even be able to afford a two-family home and rent out an upstairs apartment."

I waited for an answer, and it finally came.

"Maybe I should just sleep on that one... It would be quite a change for us."

"Not really," I said. "Anyway, we're just discussing possibilities. Let's ADD up Choice number four... to take out a second mortgage on your home. What are the Advantages of this choice?"

"Well," Jane deliberated, "this would give me the opportunity to both repair and invest, which will increase the value of my home and earn me interest or dividends from the investment."

"Right, and investment dividends may help pay the costs of the second mortgage... Meanwhile, the repaired home will be safer and, perhaps, improve your chances for a healthier, more secure existence."

"The house will certainly be more liveable and comfortable," Jane agreed.

"In other words," I summed up, "it will give you a feeling

of financial and personal security."

"That's about it!" she said. "But I'm sure there are disadvantages to this choice, too."

"Of course... so let's take a look at them."

Jane glanced at her empty cup... I wondered where she stashed it. I refilled her cup again.

"O.K.," she began, between sips... "A second mortgage is a loan which must be repaid, beginning almost immediately. But my investment may not yield the expected dividends, and even the principle may be lost if the investment turns sour..."

"You're getting pretty good at this," I smiled.

"Fine, but how can I get out of this mess?"

"Develop some New Ideas," I answered. "For example, you might consider adding on another room or two to your home that you can rent out, or maybe fix up the garage and turn it into a small apartment, an office or studio of some kind... You might be able to generate an additional monthly income that way."

"That's a good idea," Jane admitted, "or maybe I can turn the basement into a kitchen for a home catering service. My cousin likes to decorate cakes and make up sandwiches for small parties... She does it out of her four room apartment, and her place always looks like a tornado went through it..."

"There you go!" I exclaimed. I liked her sudden enthusiasm.

"But..." Jane frowned.

"But what?... Tell me..." I became apprehensive. She had been doing so well.

"Well," she said, "Jack can't stay away from cake, so if he knows there are lots of them downstairs, and he smells the stuff, I don't know... it could be a disaster."

"Tell me... which does Jack like more... money or cake?"

She smiled. "I think he'd sell his grandfather's stuffed grouse for a fifty dollar bill, even though it's a family heirloom."

"Well," I continued, "those cakes will bring in money... I don't think he'd want to eat up the profits."

"I think you're right," Jane agreed.

"O.K., now that that's settled, you're ready to determine which of the four choices we've ADDed up offers the best solution to your problem. Just go over your results and, based on the evidence of which choice has the most Advantages and the least Disadvantages, your best course of action will be clear."

"I see what you mean," Jane said, back on the track again. "Just thinking back of what we've discussed, I'd guess that Choice number four... to take out a second mortgage on my home, fits the bill."

"You're right," I agreed, "My notes show that this choice has more Advantages than the others, as well as less Disadvantages. Let's go with that one and see what happens..."

"O.K., where do we go from here?"

"To Step Four of the Five-Minute Problem Solver...

OWN
or consider Other's Wishes and Needs..."

"Like Jack's?" Jane asked. "Do I have to?"

"If you don't, your whole course of action may fail... It's important to ask yourself how this choice will affect others with whom you share your life."

"Well," Jane countered, "since taking out a second mortgage will enable us to make the needed repairs as well as invest, I'd say we'd both benefit from this choice."

"You may think so," I warned, "but I want you to put yourself in Jack's place and try to figure out his reaction to your plan of action. Present him with all the facts, as well as the Advantages and Disadvantages you have listed for each choice, and see if he agrees with your decision. Since you're presenting it logically..."

"Hah!" Jane interrupted, chuckling, "Me being logical will be a big surprise to Jack... He thinks I'm empty-headed all the time."

"Anyway," I ignored her remark and continued, "Compare his thoughts with yours... but be prepared; he might have some reservations against investing... He might consider it gambling, for example."

"I see."

"Now, isn't it possible that a difference of opinion such as this might upset your plans? And if it does, is there anything you can do about it?'' I asked.

"Divorce him?''

"It may not have to be that drastic... If Jack is against investing, you have three options... First, go ahead and invest anyway...''

"And have him divorce me?''

"No, nothing like that either. The second option is... don't invest.''

"Then there's the third option,'' I continued, "Do invest, but in safe bank Certificates of Deposits or government bonds... which may limit your dividends but keep the peace... Jack probably won't consider this gambling.''

"O.K., but which option shall I try?''

"Go ahead and ADD up each of the three options I've mentioned to see which is the best one to go with.''

"Fine... Now that I've straighted Jack out, what next?''

"Let's proceed with...

WIN

or What Is Needed which, as you remember, is Step Five of the Five-Minute Problem Solver... How will you go about accomplishing your choice of action?''

"Well,'' Jane began, "since my choice is getting a second mortgage on the house, I'll have to get all the information, applications, and materials necessary to apply.''

"Good... then what?''

"Then I'll list all the procedures necessary, such as... (1) getting the agreement of all family members, especially Jack's, because he'll have to co-sign the application... (2) collect all documents and forms necessary for the application. Then...'' Jane stopped, frowning.

"Then you list all materials necessary,'' I prompted. "In this case, all information such as financial and credit statements, the original mortgage, and any other documents and forms required.''

"That sounds like a lot of work.''

"I'm sure Jack can help quite a bit with that. Besides,'' I reassured her, "it's not half as bad as you think if you're organized. The way to accomplish that is with Step Six of the

Five-Minute Problem Solver... to get...

SET

with Sequence, Expense and Time."

"I'm confused," Jane stated.

"It's easy... just try to concentrate, and follow the proper Sequence," I stressed. "First, we summarize What Is Needed in correct order... Collect all documents necessary for the second mortgage application, such as your original mortgage, financial statement, updated credit information, a listing of assets and liabilities, etc."

"Let me get that all down," Jane said, taking notes.

"Then go to the bank where you negotiated your original mortgage and make application for your loan."

Jane shook her head. "This is not my cup of tea... or coffee, in this case." She lifted her cup.

"Now," I continued, ignoring her comment, "there are usually no expenses or fees involved in applying for this type of loan, but it's still a good idea to set a time limit as to when to apply. Once you've decided on your choice of action, don't let any grass grow under your feet. For example, give yourself two weeks to gather all the documents and information you've listed as necessary, and then go to it!"

"Jack is good at those things... I'll let him do it."

"You can do this yourself... Listen to Step Seven of the Five-Minute Problem Solver and..."

GO

Set your Goal and list all possible Obstacles."

"Jack!"

"Hmm..." I commented. "Now, what is your goal?"

"To go home right now," Jane got up.

"Wait, " I gently pushed her back into the chair. "Obviously your goal is to make money from investments... isn't that right?"

"If you say so."

"Is your goal realistic?"

"I'm not sure anymore."

55

"Can it be achieved?"

"Who knows."

"I'd say 'yes' on both counts."

"Thank Heaven."

"What obstacles, if any," I continued, "can stand in the way?"

"I shudder to think."

"Lack of money to invest, of course, or, in this case, needing all available funds for house repairs. Using the Five-Minute Problem Solver you determined that taking out a second mortgage on your house would enable you to take advantage of both investing your money and repairing your house."

"As I mentioned previously," I continued, "the only other major obstacle might be opposition from Jack."

"I'll say!"

"If you believe in your course of action, however, you should be able to convince him that this is the best way to accomplish your goal."

"Maybe *you* should talk to him."

"It's your job. . . just follow the steps that led up to your decision and explain it all to Jack. ADD up the choices just as we did. It convinced you, didn't it?"

"Yes," Jane admitted.

"When you've got to that point, go to Step Eight of the Five-Minute Problem Solver and. . .

WRAP

it up. . . Work, Review, Affirm and Proceed. . ."

"Now you're talking," Jane perked up.

"First, Work to finalize your decision. . . Was there any other choice available to you that might work better?"

"Let's not start that again."

"Just a theoretical question," I admitted. "The answer is. . . probably not, . . . since you have to make a decision to achieve your goal, and you don't have a rich aunt to tap for an interest-free loan, your choice looks like the best one after all."

"That's better," Jane remarked.

"Now, Review this choice by briefly thinking through the steps that brought you to it.''

"O.K., I'll try that.''

"Next, after you've thought through the steps leading to your decision, Affirm to yourself that your plan of action is workable.''

"I'm really beginning to think it is!''

"Of course it is. Finally, Proceed with your decision... Go over What Is Needed, get Set, and Go!''

"I'm raring.''

"Gather all the documents and information required, and set a time and place to accomplish it.''

"You've convinced me... I'm all set now,'' Jane stated, smiling bravely.

"Not set,'' I said, "you still have to...

SECURE

YOUR GOAL, Step Nine of the Five-Minute Problem Solver, by achieving the mental and physical relaxation necessary to focus your mind on successfully solving your problem.''

"I knew there was a catch...''

"Not really. This step will make it much easier for you to accomplish your goal. Just to review quickly... The Five-Minute Problem Solver has enabled you to set your purpose firmly in your mind, decide on the best choice of action, and determine the procedures necessary to achieve it... Now it's a good idea to clear your mind, try to relax completely, and take a few deep breaths...''

I would have liked to do that an hour ago...''

Well, now's the time... Just close your eyes...''

"O.K.''

"And breathe slowly and deeply... just relax completely...''

"Boy, I needed that!'' moaned Jane.

"Now,'' I continued, "while you relax, try to focus your mind on your plan of action... Support the thought of winning your goal, End all doubts, Complete the process of relaxation by Upholding the image of success... Reward yourself for a job well done and keep up your Enthusiasm as you carry out your choice of action.''

"I'm looking forward to the 'Reward' bit.''

"Well, Jane, you've solved your problem on paper... You're convinced it's the right thing to do, and determined the correct way of going about it. Now, get out there and translate this blueprint for success into a practical achievement... Good luck!"

"Wow, I didn't know I had this natural ability to solve a problem so easily."

"You may not have solved it naturally, but you did solve it quickly," I added.

"Yeah," Jane said. "Jack doesn't know what a gem he has. Do you think I can convince him to give me a reward of something warm and fuzzy, like mink?"

"Well, that's an altogether different kind of problem... but I bet the Five-Minute Problem Solver can help you with that one, too."

Let's Solve Another Problem

The other day Mrs. Dori M.'s husband showed up at my office in a rather nervous state. He came instead of Dori, he said, because she hadn't slept a wink the night before because of the news daughter Cindy imparted to the family.

This was rather unusual, to say the least, and ordinarily I would have refused such a switch of clients. But since the news Mr. M. mentioned presented a problem which also affected my client, I decided to listen to his tale of woe.

I motioned for him to sit down, but he was so agitated he didn't even seem aware that I was already seated. So there he stood in front of my desk, his eyes two fiery slits, and stormed...

"The nerve of that kid!"

"Who?" I asked anxiously.

"Cindy, our daughter... She wants to get married, and right away, too."

DEAL

"Please sit down," I said, "it helps me to focus my attention on what you're saying."

Reluctantly he eased himself into the chair next to him.

"Dori almost died from shock," he said.

"I can imagine," I nodded sympathetically, recalling Dori's rapid and frequent lapses into depression whenever a problem presented itself.

"So," he continued, "I immediately figured she was pregnant... I was going to kill Jimmy."

I assumed this was the boyfriend.

"That would not really solve the problem," I interjected.

I felt I had to be careful what I said to this irate mass of confusion... But Mr. M., didn't even seem to hear me.

"Luckily for both of them... Cindy told me she was O.K., I mean not pregnant."

"That's a relief," I sighed, and meant it, for both of us.

"So why do they have to be in such a hurry to get married?...

because they are so much in love and can't wait! Besides, Jimmy's cousin with whom he lives is moving out of town. So Jimmy has to move in with us."

"That sounds like a definite complication."

"Complication!" shouted Mr. M., "It's a catastrophe."

"Maybe not," I said, trying to calm him. "There's always a way."

"No there isn't," he continued, "because there isn't enough money. Cindy doesn't work and Jimmy delivers groceries after school. That's gonna make him a millionaire overnight. If not for my mother-in-law's social security checks we'd be in big trouble. I can't work my usual hours the past few months because of my back injury. But, let me tell you, we're earning those checks in aggravation... the old lady lives with us! If Jimmy moves in with us now, we won't make it. He's a growing elephant, over six feet both ways... and he has three or four helpings of everything he eats... then he cleans up what Cindy leaves on her plate. I love my wife's cooking but I only get to sample it and he gets to eat it..."

"That's not fair," I admitted.

"Wait, there's more," he continued, "Did Dori tell you we only have one bathroom and either Cindy or the old lady are always in it? Now, if Jimmy becomes a permanent guest... we'll have to draw lots."

"I'm sure we can work this out," I suggested.

"I don't know what I did wrong," he exclaimed, not even hearing me, "I always thought Cindy would graduate high school, maybe go to college... meet some nice guy with a good job, get married and move out so we could have a little more comfort... Instead Jimmy is moving in. What did I do to deserve this?"

"Let's not panic," I reassured him, "we can deal with this."

"How?"

"To begin with, let's pin down the problem."

DEFINE

"The problem is I can't afford Jimmy."

"You mean you can't have Jimmy moving in with you."

"Right!"

KEY THOUGHT

"So that's your problem... Now, your Key Thought is that the couple don't have enough money to live on their own."

"That's beside the point."

"No, it is the point... because if they had enough money to get a place of their own, you'd have no problem. Then again, if you had enough money to help them out so that they could live by themselves, there would also be no problem."

"That's true."

"So, you have two separate factors to look at..."

"Yeah, well they all add up to the same thing... I'm broke!"

"Let's see how we can begin to...

COPE

with this situation... To begin with, let's examine your choices."

"You mean I actually have some?"

"Definitely... there are always choices."

"Well, I can't see any, except Dori and I moving out and leaving the three of them to fend for themselves... But then where would we go?"

"Well, that's a definite possibility... Maybe we should look at it."

"No, no! The home would go to rack and ruin and they'd all starve... Forget that!"

"Allright... then let's go for some other choices."

"What, for instance?"

"Well, for one, you can have them live with you... and we'll figure out how."

"I'd like to see that...," he laughed dryly.

"You also have the choice of refusing to let them live with you."

"I can't do that to Cindy... Where will she go?"

"You have a third choice... You can allow them to live with you for a limited time only, until he finishes high school and gets a better job or an extra job...

"Or how about a fourth choice... You can insist that Jimmy drop out of school now and get another job...

"And, of course, number five... you can ask them to postpone the marriage until after graduation...

"Then again, there's a sixth choice... This might be a good time to build on an additional living area for the couple to occupy after graduation... In fact, maybe Jimmy and you can do most of the work yourselves..."

"You know," he commented, "that's a possibility. Maybe I could take out a small loan or a second mortgage to add on or build a carport, and turn the garage into a small apartment with a bathroom..."

ADD

"Well," I continued, "at least we've got some choices, opportunities and possibilities to work with... Why don't we examine the Advantages and Disadvantages to all these choices, and, who knows, you might even come up with some completely new and different ideas..."

"I'll probably come up with more gray hairs, or maybe I'll even go bald from worry..."

"That's what we want to avoid... so let's go about this calmly and logically."

"Easy for you to say..."

"It may seem that way to you," I said, "but I have problems too... However, I discovered a better way to solve them and I'm going to show you how... I call it The Five-Minute Problem Solver..."

"You mean it will take only five minutes to solve a problem?"

"Yes, once you learn how to use it."

"So, let's get at it," he said, eagerly.

"O.K., let's examine Choice number one, ... what can happen if they live with you now?"

"I'll go broke!"

"Let's consider possible Advantages... First of all, Jimmy could be of help to you in rearranging things to accommodate his belongings."

"Yeah, but first we have to figure out where we can put them."

"Well, you can draw up a plan of each room and see where a dresser or a chest might fit to house his things..."

"I suppose I could."

"Besides," I continued, "he could be a help in an emergency... an extra hand if someone were ill or something had to be fixed."

"I guess so," he admitted. "I don't know how handy he is but I could teach him a few things."

"And if they stayed with you, he'd owe you... You could ask for future help and you'd keep good will between the two families."

"Yeah, but what about the extra costs?"

"We'll get to that... but first, let's take a look at the Disadvantages. What are they?"

"That's easy," he said.

"Name a few."

"Well, it'll be crowded, for one thing. Second, it'll be inconvenient all around,... including, third, lack of privacy. Fourth, there are the additional costs, which, fifth, I don't have the money to pay for."

"I can think of a couple more," I continued. "They may become more dependent on you, and what about their personal initiative?"

"That's true," he agreed. "They'll get used to having the old man support them... They may never want to leave."

"Can you think of any other ideas that might change the picture?"

"What do you mean?"

"Well," I said, "what if you could come up with an idea that might help financially?"

"I see what you mean..." he replied thoughtfully. "Dori is pretty handy with a sewing machine... maybe she and Cindy could take in some sewing to make extra money... or maybe Jimmy could do odd jobs on the weekends..."

"See, that would change the picture..."

"Yeah,... I guess I could do odd jobs on weekends, too..."

"That's great," I commented. "I'm sure if you talked these ideas over with the family... other ideas would come up."

"Maybe..."

"O.K., let's examine the other choices we mentioned...

Remember the second one? You can refuse to have them live with you.''

"I don't know about that one," he said, shaking his head.

"Let's just look at it," I continued. "We can rule out anything that proves to be disadvantageous. After all, that's the purpose of this exercise. Are there any Advantages to this choice?''

"Well, I guess we'd have privacy... we'd be less crowded and the kids would learn to be independent a lot faster... but I still don't like that choice.''

"What would the Disadvantages be if you refused to have them live with you?''

He took a deep breath.

"I don't think they're mature enough to handle living by themselves... and facing the financial responsibilities... What kind of a place could they afford? A cold-water flat? They'll only get sick and then what?''

"And what will all this mean to you?''

"Certainly no peace of mind... I'll constantly worry, and Cindy will resent me and I don't want that!''

"I understand," I agreed.

"Besides, if they quit school... they'll never have a chance in life.''

"Any other thoughts or ideas?''

"Well, it would disrupt our family life to refuse to have them live with us... because we'd all be divided on that decision. Everybody would blame everybody else... it would be a worse mess than having them stay with us...''

"What if you forbid your daughter to marry?'' I asked.

"You are kidding!'' he laughed... "She'd make our lives miserable and then she'd just get into trouble... get pregnant maybe... and quit school for good. Then starts the resentment and anger.''

"O.K.," I said, "let's look at Choice number three... allowing them to live with you for a limited time only, until Jimmy finishes high school and is able to get a better job.''

"It better be for a limited time only," he said, wryly.

"Would there be an Advantages to this choice?'' I asked.

64

"Well," he replied, squinting, "I guess we'd know it's not forever... We could set some goals and find the best way to live together."

"Anything else?"

"Yeah,... I could help them financially a bit, too. Also, we'd have a better feeling about the whole thing."

"So what are the Disadvantages?"

"The inconvenience,... but let's face it, it would keep the family together."

"What about Choice number four... if you insisted Jimmy drop out of school and get a job?" I continued.

"It would ruin his future and my daughter's, too... Besides, then they'll also need money... That would be a disaster!"

"So you don't see any Advantages to that choice?"

"Well, they might leave faster... and they'd learn independence a lot faster, but in the long run we would all lose out."

"You seem really sure of that," I smiled, satisfied with his progress in problem-solving.

"Yeah, I guess I am."

"O.K.," I continued, "let's check out Choice number five."

"Which one is that?"

"The last one we listed... where you try to persuade the couple to postpone marriage until after graduation."

"Oh, that one... Well, that would be great, if they agreed."

"Why?" I asked.

"Because it would leave things the way they are for a while... and it would give us no financial problems either. We'd all get along as before... and, besides, it would help to build the kid's self-reliance and character..."

"How do you mean that?"

"Well, by having to wait for something they want very much, they'll learn that some things are worth waiting for..."

"I see," I agreed, "Now, can you see any Disadvantages to this choice?"

"Yeah," he said, thoughtfully... "they'll have to grow up a little faster and learn that they can't have everything the way they want it all the time..."

"Maybe that's not really a Disadvantage," I suggested.

"You know," he said, "you may have a point there."

"Can you think of any other Ideas?" I asked.

"Well," he replied, "the family will have to help them with their future plans. After all, if they postpone marriage... it will be a great help to us. They'll deserve help from us in return."

"O.K.," I continued, "let's see if we can determine the best choice available... the way to do this is to add up the Advantages and Disadvantages for each. Whichever has the most Advantages and the least Disadvantages is the best course of action."

I looked over my notes.

"Well, it seems Choice number five... to persuade the couple to postpone marriage until after Jimmy graduates, seems to fit the bill... Let's pursue the choice and see where it leads us."

OWN

"Let's continue with Step 4 of The Five-Minute Problem Solver... Other's Wishes and Needs. At this stage of the game we should consider how your decision will affect your wife, mother-in-law and anyone else living with you..."

"Well, my wife will certainly agree with me... My mother-in-law could be a different matter," he mused, "the last time she agreed with me was when I told her my intentions toward her daughter were honorable, and I think that was the only time... So since my record is lousy, I won't worry about pleasing her... Besides, she'll go along with the rest of us. As far as the kids are concerned... I doubt that there'd be any problem... After all, it'll only be a matter of a year or so until Jimmy graduates... I'll just explain the Advantages of this choice."

"Suppose one or more of them disagree with your decision... What would you do?"

"I'll try to explain the steps I took that lead up to this choice... I think that would persuade them it's the best way."

"And if it didn't?"

"Well, then I'd go back to checking out any new suggestions, if they have any..."

"That's right," I agreed. "You're a fast learner... Now, how do you get started to carry out your decision? In other words, let's go to Step 5 of the Five-Minute Problem Solver... What Is Needed..."

WIN

"Well, I guess the main thing I need is persuasion... I'll tell the family what I've decided and maybe review the choices with them that led me to this decision."

"To make it more convincing," I added, "may I suggest that you ADD up all the choices in writing, just the way I did in my notes. Put it all down on paper, and then total up the Advantages and Disadvantages of each choice. Show the results to them and ask them if they agree with you on paper... If they don't, they'll have to come up with some pretty convincing agruments, won't they?"

"That's true," he agreed.

"Then you'll be putting the burden of proof on them if they want to persuade you into some other choice... and, since, I think we've pretty well exhausted all the available choices in Step 2, COPE, I doubt that they'll be able to come up with any other suggestions..."

"And if they can't... they'll have to admit that my decision is the best for all concerned."

"Theoretically, yes... but it may take them a little time to agree with you."

"Well, that's understandable," he agreed.

"Let's say they finally agree with you... what then?"

"Then we'll sit down and figure out what to do next..."

"O.K., " I said. "How will you do that?"

"I'll figure out the different things I'll have to do..."

"Then," I continued, "you're ready for Step 6 of the Five-Minute Problem Solver.

SET

or, Sequence, Expense and Time... Let's start with Sequence... that includes all the different things you'll have to do... In other words, list the steps in correct order."

"Well, first we'll have to figure out when Jimmy will graduate high school, and second, how soon after that would be the best time for the wedding. Then we'll have to arrange for an engagement party . . . my wife would never forgive me if we didn't have some kind of reception to invite family and friends . . . a small one, of course . . .

"Is that the correct order so far?"

"I think so."

"Then you'd better make up a written list."

"Sounds like a good idea," he agreed.

"What comes next?" I asked.

"Well, then I think we'd talk about plans to fix up a place for the new couple after they get married . . . either in the house or by adding on in some way . . ."

"That brings up Expense . . . how about the costs of all this?"

"If my wife had her way," he laughed, "we'd spend every cent we've got . . ."

"So that's something you'd better discuss with her and reach an agreement on . . . Also decide how much Time you have to accomplish all of this. In other words, set a time limit . . ."

"Yeah," he nodded in agreement, "we should decide when all this confusion will be over with so we can go back to a normal life again . . . if that's possible with another person living with us . . . or should I say off us?"

"It may work out fine if you follow through the right way. Don't forget . . . Jimmy will be out of school and presumably working at a better job. He should be able to help out financially until he can support himself and his wife on his own . . ."

"You're right . . . I'm sure we can make it work."

"So now you're ready to go . . ."

GO

"Go? . . . Go where?" he seemed puzzled.

"I'm talking about Step 7 of the Five-Minute Problem Solver . . . GO, or Goals and Obstacles . . . In other words, set your Goals and see if there are Obstacles . . ."

"Oh, I get it . . ." he smiled, "clever. Well, there are always obstacles when you go ahead with anything important . . .''

"There are obstacles even with unimportant things, but they don't affect us as much."

"Well, this is important!" he emphasized.

"So, let's go ahead . . . Set your Goal! What is it?"

"To solve my problem the best and quickest way possible, without disrupting everyone's life . . . and without being unfair to the youngsters."

"Well, is that realistic? I mean . . . can you achieve that?"

"Maybe . . . if nothing stands in the way."

"O.K.," I continued . . . "What can stand in the way?"

"For one thing, the kids may want to get married right away in spite of my arguments."

"What will you do then," I asked.

"Try to make them see what a mistake that would be . . . They'd never keep their minds on school-work, and we'd all be on edge trying to make sure they graduate . . ."

"Good!" I said, satisfied with his work so far.

"But I know my original decision will work out . . . they're good kids," he asserted.

"Well," I said, "it sounds to me like you're ready to . . .

WRAP

up the whole situation."

"What I'd like to wrap up is two tickets to a fun place in the sun . . ."

"Disneyland?" I asked.

"No . . . that I've got at home . . ."

"You don't really believe that?" I laughed.

"I don't know . . . Sure seems like it when I get home nights," he continued. "All the women arguing . . . sounds like the household of Daffy Duck, everyone quacking at the same time."

"Well, let's see if you can work things out to make your home a fun place, too."

"That would take a monumental imagination," he sighed.

"Not necessarily . . . By WRAPping it up I'm referring to Step 8 of the Five-Minute Problem Solver . . . Now that you've made your choice and decided the best way to solve your problem, you're ready to WRAP, or Work, Re-inforce & Proceed..."

"Sounds like I'm making progress," he said.

"Yes, you are... first, you're going to Work at making a conscious decision that your choice and goal have been finaliz-ed... then you Re-inforce that decision by making a written contract with yourself to carry out your choice of action... Set the time and place to begin... finally Proceed to act on it! Begin to carry out the steps listed... the ones you wrote down in SET... Sequence, Expense & Time..."

"Yeah," he said, "I get it!... I've decided my best choice is to persuade the kids to postpone marriage until after Jimmy graduates and gets a better job... Now I'll set the time and place to sit down with them, try to persuade them that this is the best solution to our problem and make our future plans..."

"You've got it... WRAP it up!"

"O.K.," he said, "I feel better about the whole situation now."

"So what's the next step?" I asked.

"To sit down with the kids and talk..."

"Before you do that," I continued, "let's

SECURE

your goal... I'm talking about Step Nine, the final step of the Five-Minute Problem Solver... it will help you relax and focus on the successful management of the whole situation... In other words, make it easier for you to accomplish your goal, which is, after all, to persuade the kids to postpone their marriage until they can take charge of their own lives..."

"How will relaxing help me do that?"

"By clearing your mind and relaxing completely, both physically and mentally, you'll find you can handle the problem more effectively... you'll be able to speak to the kids without aggravating yourself or them... and accomplish your purpose just the way you want..."

"So how do I relax enough to do that?"

"It's easy... just close your eyes, breathe slowly and deeply... and just relax completely."

"It's beginning to work," he agreed, a little surprised.

"Now, while you relax, focus your mind on your plan of action."

"I'm focusing..."

"Support the thought of winning your goal, End all doubts, Complete the process of relaxation by Upholding the image of success... Reward yourself for a job well done and keep up your Enthusiasm as you carry out your choice of action..."

"That's a pretty good pep talk."

"O.K., now keep that in mind and hear yourself talking to them... Anticipate what they might answer and be prepared to prove to them by the system we just used... the nine steps of the Five-Minute Problem Solver, how your solution would benefit everyone."

"Believe me... I'll work at it. I'll rehearse until then."

"Good idea," I agreed, "that's good ammunition."

"Always be prepared... that's the Boy Scout motto."

"And a good one it is... So, remember when all has been accomplished, reward yourself... do something nice for yourself."

"I'll go fishing... then have a couple of beers to celebrate the catch... then go home and get into an argument over the smelly fish not fitting in with the chocolate pudding in the fridge."

"Maybe you'd better choose another reward for yourself," I laughed... "Or just throw the fish back."

"Yeah, give them a break, too... that way they won't hear the fight."

"You are a funny man," I laughed.

"Gallow's humor!"

"Well, I know you'll work it all out... I think you've turned a corner here today."

"I hope so... Well, thanks for your help... I learned a lot."

"Great," I said, "it's always good to do things in a new way, and a better one, if possible."

71

A Business Problem

I looked up from my desk to see a tall, distinguished-looking man standing in the doorway eyeing me quizzically. I surmised this was Mr. G., my next appointment.

"May I help you?" I asked.

"I hope you can," he answered hesitantly . . . "I've been recommended to you be a client of yours who you helped through bankruptcy. How are you with live business problems?"

"Oh, I can deal with the live as well as the dead . . . and, by the way, the client didn't have to go bankrupt. He worked through his problem with Chapter 13," I smiled. "He didn't lose his credit rating after all."

"Really! The last I heard he was heading for bankruptcy," he seemed surprised.

"Well, obviously that wasn't the final decision," I commented, a little proud of myself.

"I'm glad," he said.

"Do come in, please, and have some coffee . . ."

"That sounds inviting."

He walked over to the desk and sat down in the chair opposite me.

"Please help yourself," I said, indicating the coffee pot and cups on the adjacent table.

"Aren't you having any?" he asked.

"I've just finished my third cup and I'm cutting down."

"Probably a good idea," he commented.

He poured himself a cup and took a sip.

"Hey, you make a good cup of coffee," he smiled. "I wish you'd tell my secretary how you make it."

"Thank you . . . I just follow the directions on the package or can . . . Now, you're probably not here to discuss my success with a cup of coffee . . ."

"Not exactly . . . but the coffee is a nice touch. Actually, my problem is . . . well, let me give you a quick run-down of my situation. I own a rather profitable export business in Mexican food items which I ship all over the world in cans . . . I'm now at the end of the third quarter of the fiscal year... I'll meet my annual sales projection of $9,200,000 against which I anticipate an after-tax profit of $475,000..."

"That sounds great," I said.

"I usually retain 25% of the profits in the corporation," he continued. "40% of the profits I take for my family and myself as a corporate shareholder... the remaining 40% is divided among my employees as profit-sharing. Now here is the problem... I have a chance to buy out a major competitor for $2,500,000 cash. At present, I have $1,200,000 in retained earnings. I could raise an additional $900,000 in venture capital, but I don't want to risk my personal assets by putting them into the corporation. My only source for the remaining $400,000 is the end-of-the-year profits. Now, if I take all the profits for the deal, it will leave only $75,000 retained profits in the corporation. Do you follow me so far?"

"So far," I replied, "but I wish I hadn't flunked math in the sixth grade."

"Oh," he laughed... "Well, don't worry about it now."

"I won't, especially if you can give me the details of your dilemma. With those figures you must have more than one."

"Well, right now the difficulty is that I can get along with $75,000 in retained profits if there's no major crisis... and I don't foresee any. My family won't mind... after all, they'll inherit the business. But my employees are a different matter... they expect $190,000 to be divided among themselves in profit-sharing. They depend on that money for their expenses and investments for their old age... I know that after three years the merged companies will double the profits and the profit-sharing. But in the meantime I need all the profits to pay for merger expenses, interest and principal payments. So what are my alternatives? Should I risk losing my employees or should I forget the whole deal and let my competitor sell to someone else?"

"And have a new competitor," I added.

"Right! Then again, is there another way to finance the deal... and can I involve my employees in the decision?... Is there some way to help them with their expenses since they depend on profit-sharing to cover them? So, what should I do?''

"The best you can do for yourself first, so you can handle the rest with a clearer mind... O.K., let's break this confusion down to a reasonable size so we can handle it... let's DEAL with it.''

DEAL

"All right, let's DEAL with it,'' he agreed readily.

"Do we agree that you, a prosperous businessman, have an opportunity to buy out a major competitor... But that such a move would take all the corporation's end-of-the-year retained earnings, plus the funds set aside for employee profit-sharing?''

"I guess that's putting it in a nutshell,'' he replied.

"Then,'' I continued, "let's define the real problem.''

DEFINE

"Check me out on this, please... As I see it, the problem is... should you gamble most of your business earnings as well as the employees' profit-sharing funds to buy out this major competitor, or should you forget the whole deal, and let your competitor sell out to someone else?''

I paused to let him digest this material.

"O.K., that's right... what's next?''

"To determine the KEY THOUGHT, without which you wouldn't have any problem at all.''

"And what's that?'' he asked.

"In this case... the opportunity to buy out your competitor will, hopefully, bring about increased profits and business expansion. This opportunity having presented itself creates the problem.''

"I guess that's true,'' he admitted.

"So now we can...

ELUCIDATE

Let's check out the reasons for wanting to buy out the competition... Can you give me some?''

"Well, as you said before... to increase earnings and profit.''

"Yes, that's one reason,'' I agreed. "Another might be to

prevent other competitors from gaining advantage and possibly harming your business potential. . ."

"Absolutely," he nodded.

"What else?" I looked down at my notes.

"Well," he continued, "my competitor's location and usable area might be superior to my present one."

"I see, . . ." I said, writing in my notebook. "Size and location of current facility may be insufficient for projected needs."

"I like the way you put it in such precise business terms," he commented, smiling.

"I read Fortune and The Wall Street Journal from time to time," I announced proudly.

"The Old Testament and the New, eh?" he smiled.

"How about demographic considerations in the competitor's area?" I asked.

"Might be more advantageous, too," he admitted.

"In what way?"

"His area has a higher population density and probably a greater growth potential."

"And let's not forget the prestige factor," I added, "in taking over your competitor's business."

"By all means, let's not!"

"Now that we've been able to DEAL with your problem. . . let's turn to the second step and begin to. . .

COPE

"Believe me, that's what I'm trying to do. . . and it's hard."

"We'll make it easier for you," I smiled. "Now, we'll begin to examine your

CHOICES

"Wonderful. . . Nice to know I have some."

"Oh, definitely. . . I see one right off the top of my head."

"I don't," he said, shifting his gaze to the top of my head.

"Seriously. . . buy out your competitor using all of your available funds, including business earnings and funds set aside for employee profit-sharing."

"But," he said, anxiously, "that would create. . ."

75

I put my hand to stop him.

"We're not implying that this is a final choice... just a possibility."

"O.K." He sat back in his chair.

"As a second choice you could seek out alternative financing... such as, applying for a long-term bank loan, taking a partner, or going public and selling stock. Any of these will enable you to buy out the competition without jeopardizing earnings or the employees' profit-sharing funds..."

"A possibility," he nodded, stroking his chin thoughtfully.

"Of course, the third choice... dropping the whole idea and possibly letting someone else buy out your competitor... may not be the one your are looking for."

"No, that's not what I'm looking for."

"I didn't think so... But, bear in mind the possible effects of your available choices in the light of your goals... Why did you consider this whole deal in the first place?"

"I see what you mean... my final choice has to bring me increased profits and business expansion, or it's not worth going into in the first place."

"Good! Now we're ready for Step 4 of the Five-Minute Problem Solver...

ADD

We'll list the Advantages, Disadvantages and Develop any new ideas we can think of for each of the choices we've mentioned."

"Sounds good to me."

"O.K., let's examine your first choice... buying out your competitor using any funds you can lay your hands on... no matter what or who is affected by that move... meaning earnings and employees' funds. What are the Advantages?"

"The way you put it," he replied, slightly annoyed, "I'm not sure it's a viable move..."

"No emotion, please," I said in a businesslike manner. "This concerns hard cash and business. Besides, it may be a good gamble... Let's go with it and see."

"Well, it would make it possible to have greater business success and prestige."

"There you go! What else?"

"I may get into a better demographic situation... Maybe build on an already profitable established business giving me a much greater profit... Ah... also, by combining the businesses I'll certainly establish a much broader base for expansion..."

"So... it might pay to take this drastic step."

"Well, I'm really not sure."

"I think I can add to your list... How about achieving a higher level of opportunity for creative potential... for example, combining the businesses may give you greater ability to develop new ideas, new products, better advertising campaigns, etc. And perhaps the increased physical plant would adapt much better to your future needs."

"Those are definite Advantages," he agreed, "but..."

"O.K., let's see what the Disadvantages might be..."

"Let's... In fact, I think I can come up with quite a few."

"So what are they?"

"First, it's a big gamble and I might not make the profits that would make the whole deal worthwhile at all... Secondly, I could lose faithful employees if the worst happens... Also, we didn't mention professional consultants, investment and business planning fees... They could cost a bundle... And then there's market research into the demographic factors involved... It's not all that simple. The money could be spent before I even get to the bargaining table..."

"So there are expenses to consider... but maybe you can approach this from another angle..."

"Such as...?"

"Developing some new ideas... For example, combining both businesses might lead to some ideas for diversification... create markets for new products and give you a greater tax break..."

"Hmm, well, those are valid points," he admitted.

"Can you think of anything else?"

"I don't think I can add any new ideas at this point."

"Then let's go to the second choice... seeking out alternative financing to buy out your competition. Might a loan be a possible answer?"

"Well, I hate owing money, although a loan could be spread over a five year period which might make it somewhat easier at the start, and I wouldn't have to touch earnings or funds set aside for employee profit-sharing."

"Right! And you wouldn't have to face the danger of losing your employees... Besides, your accountant would be able to deduct the interest charges on your business loan..."

"Yes... sounds good, but there's usually a hitch somewhere."

"O.K., so what are the Disadvantages on this one?"

"Well, I'd have to find a way to increase profits immediately to pay off the loan... and the competitor's location had better be good enough to give me the extra profit..."

"You just came up with the hitches," I said, smiling.

"Besides," he continued, "I don't know if the consumer market is sufficient for increased profits... and then who knows, the projected value of the business may show a negative trend over five years."

"So, if you retain professional financial and business planners..., getting the best, of course, for maximum positive results, the loan could be a good move."

"Yes, but don't forget their fees all come out of the loan, which means the amount to be borrowed must be larger..."

"True," I commented, "but that's one of the considerations necessary for such a loan. What about taking a partner?"

"That sometimes presents problems," he answered, hesitantly.

"If everything is spelled out and documented, you cut half the risk... Besides, you can eventually buy him out."

"Let's put that idea aside for awhile."

"Then how about going public? Selling stock?"

"A possibility," he said. "I'll have to check that one out thoroughly."

"Can we go on to the next choice then?"

"Certainly."

"Let's work with Choice number 3... Don't buy out your competition and let him sell to someone else."

"Well, as I said, I'm not happy about that one."

"Just check it out."

"Well... alright," he agreed, grudgingly.

"The Advantages I see here are... your funds remain intact and you'll have no loans to worry about... Also, there will be much less stress for you... Can you think of anything else?"

"Well, I guess I won't have any new problems, which I'd certainly have with the new business. Also I won't jeopardize employee relations..."

"There's merit in that."

"But I might be losing out on a good deal."

"Well, that brings us to the Disadvantages."

"So," he said, "let's continue with those."

"Alright... you already mentioned one," I commented, "how about another?"

"Yes... well, costs like rent, insurance and utilities continue to rise, and demographically negative changes might develop at the old location."

"Those are major considerations," I admitted.

"Also, there may be a declining profit trend over the next few years. If so, I and my family will have to adapt our life style to a more limited income level..."

"That's a possibility," I agreed.

"An additional consideration must be taken into account... there will certainly be depreciation and deterioration of the physical facility over the next few years..."

"So, what can you do to get around these factors?"

"Well," he said, sighing, "I guess diversification into other fields or products could offset these problems and increase profits."

"That sounds like a good alternative," I commented, smiling. "Now, you're Developing some New Ideas."

"There's still another possibility that just occurred to me."

"What's that?"

"I could borrow from the bank... but only one half the original amount I'd need, providing my employees are willing to forego half the amount of profit-sharing for a couple of years in favor of stock in the combined corporation..."

"Now, that's quite an idea... but I imagine you'd have to present this in a very accurately detailed and convincing proposal..."

"Of course," he continued, "and I'd have to bring it to a vote before I could begin to set the wheels in motion..."

"You certainly have to check all the facts and figures out with your accountants, business planners and lawyers before you even call a meeting with your employees..."

"Without question," he agreed.

"Well, we can start checking it out right here and now to see what you've got... You know, Advantages, Disadvantages and New Ideas..."

"Yes, let's do that now," he said, enthusiastically.

"What would the Advantages be?"

"Well, it would reduce the amount of the loan for one thing, so I wouldn't owe that much..."

"Good!" I nodded in approval.

"It would help to spread the responsibility because there would be more people involved..."

"Right... give your employees more involvement. In that way there's also less danger of losing them."

"Definitely."

"Anything else?"

"Not off-hand," he replied, hesitantly.

"O.K.,... Disadvantages," I prompted.

"Loss of some corporate stock-ownership and control over policy."

"Important factors," I commented.

"Yes, and there is the fact that it was always a family-owned business in the first place... Now it won't be entirely that."

"Still, on the Advantage side there is that assurance of future profit and expansion..."

"Yes, but on a large bank loan over a five year period I could have the same results..."

"So, which way do you want to go?"

"I want to leave something to my family that they can work with without anyone's permission... Once you take in a partner or sell shares or go public, the focus of control shifts and if there is another way... Let's face it, too many cooks!... as the saying goes... Anyway, I don't want my family to have to get permission from others to run a company which was the family's to begin with..."

"So..." I waited for his final statement.

"So, it's the loan over five years."

"Right," I said, "now let's work with that... Since there are no other ideas or choices, let's begin to evaluate the Advantages and Disadvantages for each choice... always bearing in mind the KEY THOUGHT... wanting to expand in order to maximize profits."

"Alright... I'd say Choice number two, alternative financing, offers the most Advantages and the least Disadvantages of all the choices we've discussed... whether a five-year bank loan or ½ bank and ½ employee funds... either could work. Of course, I'd prefer to retain complete control."

"We still have some steps to go to make sure of that."

"What else is there?"

OWN

"Other's Wishes and Needs, for one... or Step Four of the Five-Minute Problem Solver. First, your employees' approval if you want one-half their profit-sharing fund."

"True," he admitted.

"How about your spouse and other family members, O.K.?... Maybe they have some reservations or other ideas about this..."

"I don't think the family would be a problem."

"Check it out," I suggested, "you never know... Besides, you certainly have to get your accountant's and other advisor's considerations, or if you have a partner..."

"No partner!"

"What about going public?"

"Pretty much the same as selling stock to the employees for one-half the profit... only on a larger scale and more people to account to..."

"So that's out?" I asked.

"I'd say so!"

"Let's check out a partnership..."

"Don't bother... I've had the experience."

"It might really help," I urged.

"Look, I can rattle off the Advantages... More money to play with, shared responsibility, division of labor, two heads are better than one... need I go on?"

"And the Disadvantages?"

"O.K., he, or she, might not do the job right, we could disagree on how money should be spent, and the partner may not carry out assigned tasks... Anyway, in my case, I was in another business before this one, and I had one partner legally but an army off the books. Talking about checking with others... whenever a decision had to be made, my partner had to check it out with his wife, his kids, his mother-in-law, brother-in-law, his dog, the neighbors... half the contracts were lost until he made up his mind... Result? I'm in a different business now without him and his battallion of advisors..."

"No partner, then," I said, smiling. "Well, good... one headache less to worry about."

"You said it," he agreed.

"So, if all the important people in your life agree with your choice, the next step is...

WIN

What Is Needed to proceed, and we'll get right into it... Assuming now that you get a positive response to OWN, Other's Wishes and Needs, you are ready to proceed with consultation and research into the best method of obtaining alternative financing to achieve your goals..."

"That sounds like a good start," he commented.

"Secondly," I continued, "you'll need research into the demographics of your area and your competitor's area to see what factors are involved... Then you'll need a survey of your competitor's business finances, assets, etc... including financial statements and investigations... Here you would consult with your accountant and/or financial advisor."

"I'm taking notes," he said, rapidly scribbling on a piece of paper.

"Then go over your finances... Look over agreements and contracts... might as well consult with your lawyer... Last, but not least, work out your bank financing and/or other alternatives. I think I've covered most of it."

"I'd say you've come up with a pretty thorough agenda."

"I try," I said, smiling.

"Well," he sighed, "I've got my work cut out for me."

"True, but consider the end result. . ."

"I am. . . and I'm hoping this will be a big break for me."

"Well, let's continue and make certain that we cover all the bases. . . it's an important ball game."

"Oh, it is that!" he nodded in agreement.

"Let's go on to the next step in the Five-Minute Problem Solver. . .

SET

or, Sequence, Expense & Time. . . When you've gathered all the information from WIN, What Is Needed, list all of it in correct Sequence. . . Get close estimates for all Expenses in each category, namely. . . research costs, consultants' fees, lawyers' fees, costs of acquisition of new business, interest charges of bank loans over the payout period, and details of other alternatives."

"All of this is definitely time consuming," he remarked.

"Of course, but necessary steps to follow through. . . So, you estimate the Time all this will take and begin to work around it. It's important to set a goal and stick to it. You handle this as you would any other business matter. . . Now we come to. . .

GO

Goals & Obstacles. . . You know whenever you have goals you'll encounter obstacles."

"You're telling me!"

"To begin with, redefine your goal. . . Now, you tell me what it is. . ."

"You don't think I've forgotten it already?"

"No, but I want you to state it clearly and succinctly."

"I want to expand my business to increase profits. . ."

"And the best way to do this is. . .?"

"Buy out my competitor if the business qualifies, and to do it by obtaining a five-year bank loan. . . At least, that's how I see it now. But, as you said... I have to check everything out first, but on the assumption that all comes out in favor of buying... I'll go for the loan."

"So," I commented, "first, you'll find out how your family and/or business associates feel... hope there's no negativity there... secondly, you'll check the demographics... third, the costs, and finally bank financing, if approved..."

"Sounds like I'm already there."

"I hope so... Then we'll

WRAP

it up... Work, Review, Affirm, Proceed, the next step in the Five-Minute Problem Solver... Well, you still have work to do."

"Don't I know it," he admitted.

"That's a good attitude," I said. First, you must WORK at making a conscious decision that your goal and choice of action have been finalized."

"I think I've already done that."

"Good! Then REVIEW all the steps that led up to your decision... although in this case you may have to re-evaluate one or two points after you get some answers from your research. Then AFFIRM... make sure you still want this deal, and finally PROCEED... start the ball rolling."

"Sounds good!"

"Now, let me show you how to

SECURE

"How to secure?" he mused. "Interesting idea."

"Oh, it is... if you think about it. It's the final step in the Five-Minute Problem Solver. In fact, you've probably done some of this mental exercise, without realizing it, before any business deal, any idea development or any wish fulfillment... it'll be familiar to you."

"So what do I do?"

"You begin by clearing your mind and relaxing completely, both physically and mentally... then you'll find that the entire situation comes into focus... you'll be able to see the forest instead of the trees."

"How do I achieve this complete relaxation?"

"The best advice I can give you is just to forget all your problems for a while. Remember, before taking a big exam at school, you were advised to forget all about the subject and relax the night before? Of course, that was assuming you'd done your homework before."

"The memory's still vivid!"

"Well, if you've followed the previous eight steps of the Five-Minute Problem Solver you've done your homework... So, first forget the whole problem and clear you mind... Go ahead, try it as an exercise."

"It's not easy."

"I know, but try... now, begin to relax. Close your eyes, breathe slowly and deeply a few times... Do you notice a difference?"

"I think so."

"Now, while you're relaxing, begin to focus your mind on your plan of action..."

"O.K., I see pretty clearly it's the best way to go to solve my problem, and I'm sure I can handle it."

"Good... now Support the thought of achieving your goal, End all doubts, Complete the process of relaxation by Upholding the image of success, Reward yourself for a job well done and keep up your Enthusiasm as you carry out your choice of action."

"That's pretty good re-inforcement!"

"Just what it's meant to be."

"O.K., I think we've just about solved my problem... I'll get going on that research immediately..."

"Please do, but never lose sight of your goals... to expand your business in order to maximize profits. Anything that doesn't fit in with that premise has to be re-evaluated. Use the steps we've gone over today as a guidemap to your destination, but, obviously, you need more information on the terrain and you may have to make some detours to get around roadblocks..."

"That fits the situation pretty well."

"Get going then and set yourself a time limit... and stick to it. Don't let the competition get ahead of you."

"I'm going to get in touch with my accountant and lawyer tomorrow morning."

"Please let me know how things are going, and if I can be of any further help."

"I will, and thank you... I feel much more confident about the whole situation now."